AF303660

 tredition®

tredition was established in 2006 by Sandra Latusseck and Soenke Schulz. Based in Hamburg, Germany, tredition offers publishing solutions to authors and publishing houses, combined with world-wide distribution of printed and digital book content. tredition is uniquely positioned to enable authors and publishing houses to create books on their own terms and without conventional manu-facturing risks.

For more information please visit: www.tredition.com

TREDITION CLASSICS

This book is part of the TREDITION CLASSICS series. The creators of this series are united by passion for literature and driven by the intention of making all public domain books available in printed format again - worldwide. Most TREDITION CLASSICS titles have been out of print and off the bookstore shelves for decades. At tredi-tion we believe that a great book never goes out of style and that its value is eternal. Several mostly non-profit literature projects pro-vide content to tredition. To support their good work, tredition donates a portion of the proceeds from each sold copy. As a reader of a TREDITION CLASSICS book, you support our mission to save many of the amazing works of world literature from oblivion. See all available books at www.tredition.com.

Project Gutenberg

The content for this book has been graciously provided by Project Gutenberg. Project Gutenberg is a non-profit organization founded by Michael Hart in 1971 at the University of Illinois. The mission of Project Gutenberg is simple: To encourage the creation and distribu-tion of eBooks. Project Gutenberg is the first and largest collection of public domain eBooks.

The Loss of the Kent, East Indiaman, in the Bay of Biscay Narrated in a Letter to a Friend

Duncan McGregor

Imprint

This book is part of TREDITION CLASSICS

Author: Duncan McGregor
Cover design: Buchgut, Berlin – Germany

Publisher: tredition GmbH, Hamburg - Germany
ISBN: 978-3-8472-1255-3

www.tredition.com
www.tredition.de

ESCAPING FROM THE BURNING SHIP.

THE LOSS
OF THE
KENT EAST INDIAMAN
IN THE BAY OF BISCAY.

NARRATED IN A LETTER TO A FRIEND

BY

General Sir DUNCAN MACGREGOR, K.C.B.

NEW EDITION, WITH ADDITIONS.

THE RELIGIOUS TRACT SOCIETY,

56, Paternoster Row; 65, St. Paul's Churchyard;
and 164, Piccadilly.

AUTHOR'S NOTE.

The older I grow, and I am now in my 94th year, I am the more convinced of the special interposition of Divine Providence in the winter recorded, in the following Tract.

[Pg 7]

The Author

THE LOSS OF THE KENT EAST INDIAMAN.

My Dear E— —,

You are aware that the *Kent*, Captain Henry Cobb, a fine new ship of 1,350 tons, bound to Bengal and China, left the Downs on the 19th of February, with 20 officers, 344 soldiers, 43 women, and 66 children, belonging to the 31st regiment; with 20 private passengers, and a crew (including officers) of 148 men—in all, 641 persons on board.

The bustle attendant on a departure for India is calculated to sub-due the force of those deeply painful sensations to which few men can refuse to yield, in the immediate prospect of a long and distant separation from the land of their fondest and earliest recollections. With my [Pg 8] gallant shipmates, indeed, whose elasticity of spirits is remarkably characteristic of the professions to which they be-longed, hope appeared greatly to predominate over sadness. Sur-rounded as they were by every circumstance that could render their voyage propitious, and in the ample enjoyment of every necessary that could contribute either to their health or their comfort, their hearts seemed to beat high with contentment and gratitude towards that country which they zealously served, and whose interests they were cheerfully going forth to defend.

With a fine fresh breeze from the north-east, the stately *Kent*, in bearing down the Channel, speedily passed many a well-known spot on the coast dear to our remembrance; and on the evening of the 23rd we took our last view of happy England, and entered the wide Atlantic, without the expectation of again seeing land until we reached the shores of India.

With slight interruptions of bad weather, we continued to make way until the night of Monday, the 28th, when we were suddenly arrested in lat. 47° 30′, long. 10°, by a violent gale from the south-west, which [Pg 9] gradually increased during the whole of the following morning.

To those who have never "gone down to the sea in ships, and seen the wonders of the Lord in the great deep," or even to such as have never been exposed in a westerly gale to the tremendous swell in the Bay of Biscay, I am sensible that the most sober description of the magnificent spectacle of "watery hills in full succession flowing" would appear sufficiently exaggerated. But it is impossible, I think, for the inexperienced mariner, however unreflecting he may try to be, to view the effects of the increasing storm, as he feels his solitary vessel reeling to and fro under his feet, without involuntarily raising his thoughts, with a secret confession of helplessness and veneration that he may never before have experienced, towards that Being whose power, under ordinary circumstances, we may have disregarded, and whose incessant goodness we are prone to requite with ingratitude.

The activity of the officers and seamen of the *Kent* appeared to keep ample pace with that of the gale. Our larger sails were speedily taken in or closely reefed; and about ten o'clock on the morning of the 1st of March, after having struck our top-gallant yards, we were lying to, [Pg 10] under a triple-reefed maintop-sail only, with the deadlights in, and with the whole watch of soldiers attached to the life lines, that were run along the deck for this purpose.

The rolling of the ship, which was vastly increased by a dead weight of some hundred tons of shots and shell that formed a part of its lading, became so great about half-past eleven or twelve o'clock, that our main chains were thrown by every lurch considerably under water; and the best cleated articles of furniture in the cabins and the cuddy were dashed about with so much noise and violence as to excite the liveliest apprehensions of individual danger.

It was a little before this period that one of the officers of the ship, with the well-meant intention of ascertaining that all was fast below, descended with two of the sailors into the hold, where they carried with them, for safety, a light in the patent lantern; and seeing that the lamp burned dimly, the officer took the precaution to hand it up to the orlop deck to be trimmed. Having afterwards discovered one of the spirit casks to be adrift, he sent the sailors for some billets of wood to secure it; but the ship in their absence having made a heavy lurch, the [Pg 11] officer unfortunately dropped the light; and letting go his hold of the cask in his eagerness to recover the lantern, it suddenly stove, and the spirits communicating with the lamp, the whole place was instantly in a blaze.

I know not what steps were then taken. I myself had been engaged during the greater part of the morning in double-lashing and otherwise securing the furniture in my cabin, and in occasionally going to the cuddy, where the marine barometers were suspended, to mark their varying indications during the gale, in my journal; and it was on one of those occasions, after having read to Mrs. − −, at her request, the twelfth chapter of St. Luke, which so beautifully declares and illustrates the minute and tender providence of God, and so solemnly urges on all the necessity of continual watchfulness and readiness for the "coming of the Son of man," that I received from Captain Spence, the captain of the day, the alarming information that the ship was on fire in the afterhold. On hastening to the hatchway, whence smoke was slowly ascending, I found Captain Cobb and other officers giving orders, which seemed to be promptly [Pg 12] obeyed by the seamen and troops, who used every exertion by means of the pumps, buckets of water, wet sails, hammocks, &c., to extinguish the flames.

With a view to excite among the ladies as little alarm as possible, in conveying this intelligence to Colonel Fearon, the commanding officer of the troops, I knocked gently at his cabin door, and expressed a wish to speak with him; but whether my countenance betrayed the state of my feelings, or the increasing noise and confusion upon deck created apprehensions amongst them that the storm was assuming a more serious aspect, I found it difficult to pacify some of the ladies by repeated assurances that no danger whatever was to be apprehended from the gale. As long as the devouring element appeared to be confined to the spot where the fire originated, and which we were assured was surrounded on all sides by the water casks, we ventured to cherish hopes that it might be subdued;

but no sooner was the light blue vapour that at first arose succeeded by volumes of thick, dingy smoke—which speedily ascending through all the four hatchways, rolled over every part of the ship—than all further [Pg 13] concealment became impossible, and almost all hope of preserving the vessel was abandoned. "The flames have reached the cable tier," was exclaimed by some individuals, and the strong pitchy smell that pervaded the deck confirmed the truth of the exclamation.

In these awful circumstances, Captain Cobb, with an ability and decision that seemed to increase with the imminence of the danger, resorted to the only alternative now left him, of ordering the lower decks to be scuttled, the combings of the hatches to be cut, and the lower ports to be opened, for the free admission of the waves.

These instructions were speedily executed by the united efforts of the troops and seamen; but not before some of the sick soldiers, one woman, and several children, unable to gain the upper deck, had perished. On descending to the gun deck with Colonel Fearon, Captain Bray, and one or two other officers of the 31st regiment, to assist in opening the ports, I met, staggering towards the hatchway, in an exhausted and nearly senseless state, one of the mates, who informed us that he had just stumbled over [Pg 14] the dead bodies of some individuals who must have died from suffocation, to which it was evident that he himself had almost fallen a victim. So dense and oppressive was the smoke, that it was with the utmost difficulty we could remain long enough below to fulfil Captain Cobb's wishes; which were no sooner accomplished, than the sea rushed in with extraordinary force, carrying away, in its resistless progress to the hold, the largest chests, bulk-heads, etc.

Such a sight, under any other conceivable circumstances, was well calculated to have filled us with horror; but in our natural solicitude to avoid the more immediate peril of explosion, we endeavoured to cheer each other, as we stood up to our knees in water, with the faint hope that by these violent means we might be speedily restored to safety. The immense quantity of water that was thus introduced into the hold had indeed the effect, for a time, of checking the fury of the flames; but the danger of sinking having increased as the risk of explosion was diminished, the ship became water-logged, and presented other indications of settling previous to her going down. [Pg 15]

Death in two of its most awful forms now encompassed us, and we seemed left to choose the terrible alternative. But always preferring the more remote, though equally certain crisis, we tried to shut the ports again, to close the hatches, and to exclude the external air, in order, if possible, to prolong our existence, the near and certain termination of which appeared inevitable.

The scene of horror that now presented itself baffles all description;—

"Then rose from sea to sky the wild farewell;
Then shrieked the timid, and stood still the brave."

The upper deck was covered with between six and seven hundred human beings, many of whom, from previous sea-sickness, were forced, on the first alarm, to flee from below almost in a state of nakedness, and were now running about in quest of husbands, children, or parents. While some were standing in silent resignation, or in stupid insensibility to their impending fate, others were yielding themselves up to the most frantic despair. Some on their knees were earnestly imploring, with significant gesticulations and in noisy supplications, the mercy [Pg 16] of Him whose arm, they exclaimed, was at length outstretched to smite them; others were to be seen hastily crossing themselves, and performing the various external acts required by their peculiar persuasion; while a number of the older and more stout-hearted soldiers and sailors sullenly took their seats directly over the magazine; hoping, as they stated, that by means of the explosion which they every instant expected, a speedier termination might be put to their sufferings. [1] Several of the soldiers' wives and children, who had fled for temporary shelter into the after cabins on the upper decks, were engaged in prayer and in reading the Scriptures with the ladies; some of whom were enabled, with wonderful self-possession, to offer to others those spiritual consolations which a firm and intelligent trust in the Redeemer of the world appeared at this awful hour to impart to their own breasts. The dignified deportment of two young [Pg 17] ladies, [2] in particular, formed a specimen of natural strength of mind, finely modified by Christian feeling, that failed not to attract the notice and admiration of every one who had an opportunity of witnessing it. On the melancholy announcement being made to them that all hope must be relinquished, and that death was rapidly and inevitably approaching, one of the ladies above referred to, calmly sinking down on her knees, and clasping her hands together, said, "Even so, come, Lord Jesus," and immediately proposed to read a portion of the Scriptures to those around her. Her sister with nearly equal composure and collectedness of mind selected the forty-sixth and other appropriate Psalms, which were accordingly read, with intervals of prayer, by those ladies alternately to the assembled females.

One young gentleman, of whose promising talents and piety I dare not now make further mention, having calmly asked me my opinion respecting the state of the ship, I told him that I thought we should be prepared to sleep that night in eternity; and I [Pg 18] shall never forget the peculiar fervour with which he replied, as he pressed my hand in his, "My heart is filled with the peace of God;" adding, "yet, though I know it is foolish, I dread exceedingly the last struggle."

Amongst the numerous objects that struck my observation at this period I was much affected with the appearance and conduct of some of the dear children, who, quite unconscious, in the cuddy cabins, of the perils that surrounded them, continued to play as usual with their little toys in bed, or to put the most innocent and unseasonable questions to those around them. To some of the older children, who seemed fully alive to the reality of the danger, I whispered, "Now is the time to put in practice the instructions you used to receive at the Regimental School, and to think of that Saviour of whom you have heard so much." They replied, as the tears ran down their cheeks, "Oh, sir, we are trying to remember them, and we are praying to God."

The passive condition to which we were all reduced by the total failure of our most strenuous exertions, while it was well calculated, and probably designed, to convince us afterwards that our deliverance was [Pg 19] effected, not by our own might or power, but by the Spirit of the Lord, afforded us ample room at the moment for deep and awful reflection, which, it is to be earnestly wished, may have been improved, as well by those who were eventually saved as by those who perished.

It has been observed by the author of the Retrospect, that "in the heat of battle, it is not only possible but easy to forget death, and cease to think; but in the cool and protracted hours of a shipwreck, where there is often nothing to engage the mind but the recollection of tried and unsuccessful labours, and the sight of unavoidable and increasing harbingers of destruction, it is not easy or possible to forget ourselves or a future state."

The general applicability of the latter part of this proposition I am disposed to doubt; for if I were to judge of the feelings of all on board by those of the number who were heard to express them, I should apprehend that a large majority of those men, whose previous attention has never been fairly and fully directed to the great subject of religion, approach the gates of death, it may be with solemnity, or with terror, but without any definable or tangible conviction of the fact that after death cometh the judgment. [Pg 20]

Several there were who vowed in loud and piteous cries, that if the Lord God would spare their lives, they would thenceforward dedicate all their powers to His service; and not a few were heard to exclaim, in the bitterness of remorse, that the judgments of the Most High were justly poured out upon them for their neglected Sabbaths, and their profligate or profane lives; but the number of those was extremely small who appeared to dwell either with lively hope or dread on the view of an opening eternity. And as a further evidence of the truth of this observation, I may mention that when I afterwards had occasion to mount the mizen shrouds, I there met with a young man, who had brought me a letter of introduction from our excellent friend, Dr. G—n, to whom I felt it my duty, while we were rocking on the mast, quietly to propose the great question, "What must we do to be saved?" and this young gentleman has since informed Mr. P. that though he was at that moment fully persuaded of the certainty of immediate death, yet the subject of eternity, in any form, had not once flashed upon his mind previous to my conversation.

While we thus lay in a state of physical [Pg 21] inertion, but with all our mental faculties in rapid and painful activity—with the waves lashing furiously against the sides of our devoted ship, as if in anger with the hostile element for not more speedily performing its office of destruction,—the binnacle, by one of those many lurches which were driving everything movable from side to side of the vessel, was suddenly wrenched from its fastenings, and all the apparatus of the compass dashed to pieces upon the deck; on which one of the young mates, emphatically regarding it for a moment, cried out with the emotion so natural to a sailor under such circumstances, "What! is the *Kent's* compass really gone?" leaving the bystanders to form, from that omen, their own conclusions. One promising young officer of the troops was seen thoughtfully removing from his writing-case a lock of hair, which he composedly deposited in his bosom; and another officer procuring paper and pens, addressed a short communication to his father, which was afterwards carefully enclosed in a bottle, in the hope that it might eventually reach its destination, with the view, as he stated, of relieving him from the long years of fruitless anxiety and suspense [Pg 22] which our melancholy fate would awaken, and of bearing his humble testimony, at a moment when his sincerity could scarcely be questioned, to the faithfulness of that God in whose mercy he trusted, and whose peace he largely enjoyed in the tremendous prospect of immediate dissolution. [3] It was at this appalling instant, when "all hope that we should be saved was then taken away," and when the letter referred to was about being committed to the waves, that it occurred to Mr. Thomson, the fourth mate, to send a man to the fore-top, rather with the ardent wish than the expectation, that [Pg 25] [Pg 24] [Pg 23] some friendly sail might be discovered on the face of the waters. The sailor, on mounting, threw his eyes round the horizon for a moment—a moment of unutterable suspense—and waving his hat exclaimed, "A sail on the lee bow!" The joyful announcement was received with deep-felt thanksgivings, and with three cheers, upon deck. Our flags of distress were instantly hoisted, and our minute guns fired; and we endeavoured to bear down under our three top-sails and fore-sail upon the stranger, which afterwards proved to be the *Cambria*, [4] a small brig of 200 tons burden, Captain Cook, bound to Vera Cruz, having on board twenty or

thirty Cornish miners, and other agents of the Anglo-Mexican
Company.

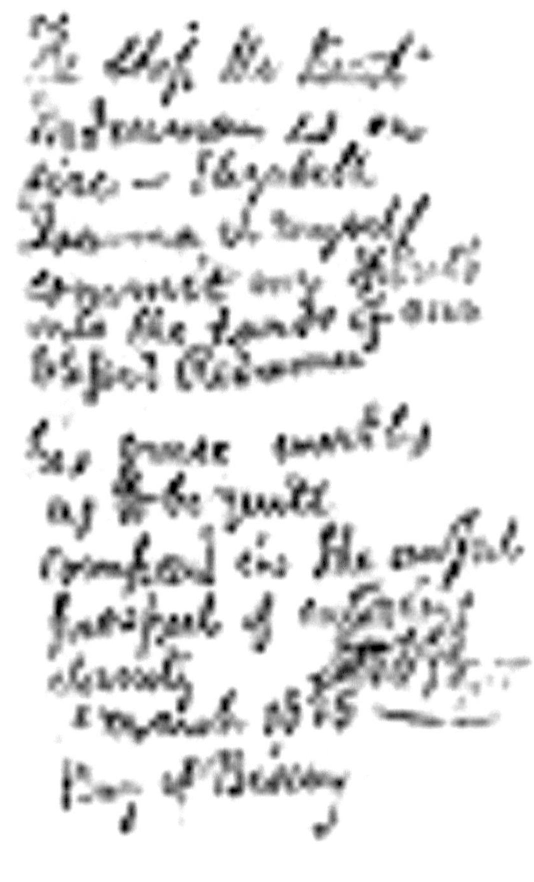

View larger image

For ten or fifteen minutes we were left in doubt whether the crew of the brig perceived our signals, or perceiving them, were either [Pg 26] disposed or able to lend us any assistance. From the violence of the gale, it seems that the report of our guns was not heard; but the ascending volumes of smoke from the ship sufficiently announced the dreadful nature of our distress; and we had the satisfaction, after a short period of dark suspense, to see the brig hoist British colours, and crowd all sail to hasten to our relief.

Although it was impossible, and would have been improper, to repress the rising hopes that were pretty generally diffused amongst us by the unexpected sight of the *Cambria*, yet I confess, that when I reflected on the long period our ship had been already burning — on the tremendous sea that was running — on the extreme smallness of the brig, and the immense number of human beings to be saved, I could only venture to hope that a few might be spared; but I durst not for a moment contemplate the possibility of my own preservation.

SAVED FROM THE WRECK.

While Captain Cobb, Colonel Fearon, and Major MacGregor of the 31st regiment, were consulting together, as the brig was approaching us, on the necessary preparations for getting out the boats, etc., one of the officers asked Major MacGregor in what [Pg 29] [Pg 28] [Pg 27] order it was intended the officers should move off; to which the other replied, "Of course in funeral order;" which injunction was instantly confirmed by Colonel Fearon, who said, "Most undoubtedly, the juniors first; but see that any man is cut down who presumes to enter the boats before the means of escape are presented to the women and children."

To prevent the rush to the boats as they were being lowered, which, from certain symptoms of impatience manifested both by soldiers and sailors, there was reason to fear, some of the military officers were stationed over them with drawn swords. But from the firm determination which these exhibited, and the great subordination observed, with few exceptions, by the troops, this proper precaution was afterwards rendered unnecessary.

Arrangements having been made by Captain Cobb for placing in the first boat, previous to letting it down, all the ladies, and as many of the soldiers' wives as it could safely contain, they hurriedly wrapped themselves up in whatever articles of clothing could be found; and I think about two, or half-past two o'clock, a most mournful pro [Pg 30] cession advanced from the after cabins to the starboard cuddy port, outside of which the cutter was suspended. Scarcely a word was uttered—not a scream was heard—even the infants ceased to cry, as if conscious of the unspoken and unspeakable anguish that was at that instant rending the hearts of their parting parents; nor was the silence of voices in any way broken, except in one or two cases, where the ladies plaintively entreated permission to be left behind with their husbands. But on being assured that every moment's delay might occasion the sacrifice of a human life, they successively suffered themselves to be torn from the tender embrace, and with that fortitude which never fails to characterize and adorn their sex on occasions of overwhelming trial, were placed, without a murmur, in the boat, which was immediately lowered into a sea so tempestuous as to leave us only to hope against hope that it should live in it for a single moment. Twice the cry was heard from those on the chains that the boat was swamping. But He who enabled the apostle Peter to walk on the face of the deep, and was graciously attending to the earnest aspirations of those on board, had decreed its safety. [Pg 31]

Although Captain Cobb had used every precaution to diminish the danger of the boat's descent, by stationing a man with an axe to cut away the tackle from either extremity, should the slightest difficulty occur in unhooking it; yet the peril attending the whole operation, which can only be adequately estimated by nautical men, had very nearly proved fatal to its numerous inmates.

After one or two unsuccessful attempts to place the little frail bark fairly upon the surface of the water, the command was at length given to unhook; the tackle at the stern was, in consequence, immediately cleared; but the ropes at the bow having got foul, the sailor found it impossible to obey the order. In vain was the axe applied to the entangled tackle; the moment was inconceivably critical, as the boat, which necessarily followed the motion of the ship, was gradually rising out of the water, and must, in another instant, have been hanging perpendicularly by the bow, and its helpless passengers launched into the deep, had not a most providential wave suddenly struck and lifted up the stern, so as to enable the seamen to disengage the tackle. The boat being thus dexterously cleared from the ship, [Pg 32] was seen after a while from the poop, battling with the billows,—now raised, in its progress to the brig, like a speck on their summit, and then disappearing for several seconds, as if engulfed "in the horrid vale" between them. [5]

The *Cambria* having prudently lain to at some distance from the *Kent*, lest she should be involved in her explosion, or exposed to the fire from her guns, which, being all shotted, afterwards went off as the flames successively reached them, the men had a considerable way to row; and the success of this first experiment seeming to be the measure of our future hopes, the movements of this precious boat—incalculably precious, without doubt, to the agonized husbands and fathers immediately connected with it—were watched with intense anxiety by all on board.

The better to balance the boat in the raging sea through which it had to pass, and to enable the seamen to ply their oars, the women and children were stowed promis [Pg 33] cuously under the seats, and consequently exposed to the risk of being drowned by the continual dashing of the spray over their heads, which so filled the boat during the passages that before their arrival at the brig the poor females were sitting up to the waist in water, and their children kept with the greatest difficulty above it.

However, in the course of twenty minutes the little cutter was seen alongside the ark of refuge; and the first human being that happened to be admitted, out of the vast assemblage that ultimately found shelter there, was the infant son of Major MacGregor, a child of only a few weeks old, who was caught from his mother's arms and lifted into the brig by Mr. Thomson, the fourth mate of the *Kent*, the officer who had been ordered to take charge of the ladies' boat. [6]

But the extreme difficulty and danger presented to the women and children in getting into the *Cambria* seemed scarcely less imminent than that which they had previously encountered; for to prevent the boat from swamping or being stove against the side of the brig, while its passengers were disem [Pg 34] barking, required no ordinary exercise of skill and perseverance on the part of the sailors, and of self-possession and effort on that of the females themselves. On coming alongside of the *Cambria*, Captain Cook very judiciously called first for the children, who were successively thrown or handed up from the boat. The women were then urged to avail themselves of every favourable heave of the sea by springing towards the many friendly arms that were extended from the vessel to receive them; and, notwithstanding the deplorable consequence of making a false step under such critical circumstances, not a single accident occurred to any individual belonging to the first boat. Indeed, the only one whose life appears to have been placed in extreme jeopardy alongside was one of the ladies, who, in attempting to spring from the boat, came short of the hand that was held out to her, and would certainly have perished, had she not most happily caught hold at the instant of a rope that happened to be hanging over the *Cambria's* side, to which she clung for some moments, until she was dragged into the vessel.

I have reason to know that the feelings of oppressive delight, gratitude, and praise [Pg 35] experienced by the married officers and soldiers on being assured of the comparative safety of their wives and children, so entirely abstracted their minds from their own situation as to render them for a little while totally insensible either to the storm that beat upon them, or to the active and gathering volcano that threatened every instant to explode under their feet.

It being impossible for the boats, after the first trip, to come alongside the *Kent*, a plan was adopted for lowering the women and children by ropes from the stern, by tying them two and two together. But from the heaving of the ship, and the extreme difficulty in dropping them at the instant the boat was underneath, many of the poor creatures were unavoidably plunged repeatedly under water; and much as humanity may rejoice that no woman was eventually lost by this process, yet it was as impossible to prevent, as it was deplorable to witness, the great sacrifice thus occasioned of the younger children—the same violent means which only reduced the parents to a state of exhaustion or insensibility, having entirely extinguished the vital spark in the feebler frames of the infants that were fastened to them. [Pg 36]

Amid the conflicting feelings and dispositions manifested by the numerous actors in this melancholy drama, many affecting proofs were elicited of parental and filial affection, or of disinterested friendship, that seemed to shed a momentary halo around the gloomy scene.

Two or three soldiers, to relieve their wives of a part of their families, sprang into the water with their children, and perished in their endeavours to save them. One young lady, who had resolutely refused to quit her father, whose sense of duty kept him at his post, was near falling a sacrifice to her filial devotion, not having been picked up by those in the boats until she had sunk five or six times. A man, who was reduced to the frightful alternative of losing his wife or his children, hastily decided in favour of his duty to the former. His wife was accordingly saved, but his four children, alas! were left to perish. A fine fellow, a soldier, who had neither wife nor child of his own, but who evinced the greatest solicitude for the safety of those of others, insisted on having three children lashed to him, with whom he plunged into the water; not being able to reach the boat, he was again drawn [Pg 37] into the ship with his charge, but not before two of the children had expired. One man fell down the hatchway into the flames, and another had his back so completely broken as to have been observed quite doubled falling overboard. These spectacles of individual loss and suffering were not confined to the entrance upon the perilous voyage between the two ships. One man, who fell between the boat and brig, had his head literally crushed to pieces; and some others were lost in their attempts to ascend the side of the *Cambria*.

Seeing that the tardy means employed for the escape of the women and children necessarily consumed a great deal of time that might be partly devoted to the general preservation, orders were given that along with the females, each of the boats should also admit a certain portion of the soldiers, several of whom, in their impatience to take advantage of this permission, flung themselves overboard, and sank in their ill-judged and premature efforts for deliverance.

One poor fellow of this number, a very respectable man, had actually reached the boat, and was raising his hand to lay hold on the gunwale, when the bow of the boat, [Pg 38] by a sudden pitch, struck him on the head, and he instantly went down. There was a peculiarity attending this man's case that deserves notice. His wife, to whom he was warmly attached, not having been of the allotted number of women to accompany the regiment abroad, resolved in her anxiety to follow her husband, to defeat this arrangement, and accordingly repaired with the detachment to Gravesend, where she ingeniously managed, by eluding the vigilance of the sentries, to get on board, and conceal herself for several days; and although she was discovered, and sent ashore at Deal, she contrived a second time, with true feminine perseverance, to get between decks, where she continued to secrete herself until the morning of the fatal disaster.

While the men were thus bent in various ways on self-preservation, one of the sailors, who had taken his post with many others over the magazine, awaiting with great patience the dreaded explosion, at last cried out, as if in ill-humour that his expectation was likely to be disappointed, "Well, if she won't blow up, I'll see if I can't get away from her;" and jumping up, he made his way to the boats, which he reached in safety. [Pg 39]

I ought to state that three of the six boats we originally possessed were either completely stove or swamped in the course of the day, one of them with men in it, some of whom were seen floating in the water for a moment before they disappeared; and it is suspected that one or two of those who went down must have sunk under the weight of their spoils, the same individuals having been seen eagerly plundering the cuddy cabins.

As the day was rapidly drawing to a close, and the flames were slowly but perceptibly extending, Colonel Fearon and Captain Cobb evinced an increasing anxiety to relieve the remainder of the gallant men under their charge.

To facilitate this object a rope was suspended from the extremity of the spanker-boom, along which the men were recommended to proceed, and thence slide down by the rope into the boats. But as, from the great swell of the sea, and the constant heaving of the ship, it was impossible for the boats to preserve their station for a moment, those who adopted this course incurred so great a risk of swinging for some time in the air, and of being repeatedly plunged under water, or dashed against the sides of [Pg 40] the boats underneath, that many of the landsmen continued to throw themselves out of the stern window on the upper deck, preferring what appeared to me the more precarious chance of reaching the boats by swimming. Rafts made of spars, hencoops, etc., were also ordered to be constructed, for the twofold purpose of forming an intermediate communication with the boats—a purpose, by the bye, which they very imperfectly answered—and of serving as a last point of retreat, should the further extension of the flames compel us at once to desert the vessel. Directions were at the same time given that every man should tie a rope round his waist, by which he might afterwards attach himself to the rafts, should he be suddenly forced to take to the water. While the people were busily occupied in adopting this recommendation, I was surprised, I had almost said amused, by the singular delicacy of one of the Irish recruits, who, in searching for a rope in one of the cabins, called out to me that he could find none except the cordage belonging to an officer's cot, and wished to know whether there would be any harm in his appropriating it to his own use. [Pg 41]

The gradual removal of the officers was at the same time commenced, and was marked by a discipline the most rigid, and an intrepidity the most exemplary; none appearing to be influenced by a vain and ostentatious bravery, which, in cases of extreme peril, affords rather a presumptive proof of secret timidity than of fortitude; nor any betraying an unmanly or unsoldierlike impatience to quit the ship; but, with the becoming deportment of men neither paralyzed by, nor profanely insensible to, the accumulating dangers that encompassed them, they progressively departed in the different boats with their soldiers; those who happened to proceed first leaving behind them an example of coolness that could not be unprofitable to those who followed.

But the finest illustration of their conduct was displayed in that of their chief, whose ability and presence of mind, under the complicated responsibility and anxiety of a commander, husband, and father, were eminently calculated, throughout this dismal day, to inspire all others with composure and fortitude. Never for one moment did Colonel Fearon seem to forget the authority with which his sovereign had invested him, nor [Pg 42] did any of his officers—as far as my observation went—cease to remember the relative situations in which they were severally placed. Even in the gloomiest moments of that dark season, when the dissolution of every earthly distinction seemed near at hand, the decision and confidence with which orders were issued on the one hand, and the promptitude and respect with which they were obeyed on the other, offered the best proofs of the stability of the well-connected system of discipline established in the 31st regiment, and the most unquestionable ground for the high and flattering commendation which his Royal Highness, the Commander-in-chief, has been pleased to bestow upon it.

I should, however, be guilty of injustice and unkindness if I here omitted to bear my humble testimony to the manly behaviour of the East India Company's cadets, and other private passengers on board, who emulated the best conduct of the officers of the ship and of the troops, and equally participated with them in all the hardships and exertions of the day.

As an agreeable proof, too, of the subordination and good feeling that governed the [Pg 43] poor soldiers in the midst of their sufferings, I ought to state that towards evening, when the melancholy groups who were passively seated on the poop, exhausted by previous fatigue, anxiety, and fasting, were beginning to experience the pain of intolerable thirst, a box of oranges was accidentally discovered by some of the men, who, with a degree of mingled consideration, respect, and affection, that could hardly have been expected at such a moment, refused to partake of the grateful beverage until they had offered a share of it to their officers.

I regret that the circumstances under which I write do not allow me sufficient time for recalling to my recollection all the busy thoughts that engaged my own mind on that eventful day, or the various conjectures which I ventured to form of what was passing in the minds of others.

But one idea was forcibly suggested to me,—that instead of being able to trace amongst my numerous associates that diversity of fortitude which I should have expected would mark their conduct—forming, as it were, a descending series, from the decided heroism exhibited by some, down to the lowest degree of pusillanimity [Pg 44] and frenzy discoverable in others,—I remarked that the mental condition of my fellow-sufferers was rather divided by a broad but, as it afterwards appeared, not impassable line; on the one side of which were ranged all whose minds were greatly elevated by the excitement above their ordinary standard; and on the other was to be seen the incalculably smaller but more conspicuous group, whose powers of acting and thinking became absolutely paralyzed, or were driven into delirium, by the unusual character and pressure of the danger.

Nor was it uninteresting to observe the curious interchange, at least externally, of strength and weakness that obtained between those two discordant parties, during the day. Some whose agitation and timidity had, in the earlier part of it, rendered them objects of pity or contempt, afterwards rose, by some great internal effort, into positive distinction for the opposite qualities; while others, remarkable at first for calmness and courage, suddenly giving way, without any fresh cause of despair, seemed afterwards to cast their minds as they did their bodies, prostrate before the danger.

It would not, perhaps, be difficult to [Pg 45] account for these apparent anomalies; but I shall content myself with simply stating the facts, adding to them one of a similar description that sensibly affected my own mind.

Some of the soldiers near me having casually remarked that the sun was setting, I looked round, and never can I forget the intensity with which I regarded his declining rays. I had previously felt deeply impressed with the conviction that that night the ocean was to be my bed; and had, I imagined, sufficiently realized to my mind, both the last struggles and the consequences of death. But as I continued solemnly watching the departing beams of the sun, the thought that that was really the very last I should ever behold, gradually expanded into reflections the most tremendous in their import. It was not, I am persuaded, either the retrospect of a past life, or the direct fear of death or of judgment, that occupied my mind at the period I allude to; but a broad, illimitable view of eternity itself, altogether abstracted from the misery or felicity that flows through it — a sort of painless, pleasureless, sleepless eternity. I know not whither the overwhelming thought would have hurried me, had I not speedily seized, as with the [Pg 46] grasp of death, on some of those sweet promises of the gospel which give to an immortal existence its only charms; and that naturally enough led back my thoughts, by means of the brilliant object before me, to the contemplation of that blessed city, "which hath no need of the sun, neither of the moon to shine in it; for the glory of God doth lighten it, and the Lamb is the light thereof."

I have been the more particular in recording my precise feelings at the period in question, because they tend to confirm an opinion which I have long entertained — in common, I believe, with others, — that we very rarely realize even those objects that seem, in our every-day speculations, to be the most interesting to our hearts. We are so much in the habit of uttering the awful words 'Almighty,' 'heaven,' 'hell,' 'eternity,' 'divine justice,' 'holiness,' etc., without attaching to them, in all their magnitude, the ideas of which such words are the symbols, that we become overwhelmed with much of the astonishment that accompanies a new and alarming discovery if, at any time, the ideas themselves are suddenly and forcibly impressed upon us; and it is, probably, this [Pg 47] vagueness of conception, experienced even by those whose minds are not altogether unexercised on the subject of religion, that enables others, devoid of all reflection whatever, to stand on the very brink of that precipice which divides the world of time from the regions of eternity, not only with apparent, but frequently, I am persuaded, with real tranquillity. How much it is to be lamented that we do not keep in mind a truth which no one can pretend to dispute, that our indifference or blindness to danger, whether it be temporal or eternal, cannot possibly remove or diminish the extent of that danger.

Some time after the shades of night had enveloped us, I descended to the cuddy, in quest of a blanket to shelter me from the increasing cold; and the scene of desolation that there presented itself was melancholy in the extreme. The place which, only a few short hours before, had been the seat of kindly intercourse and of social gaiety, was now entirely deserted, save by a few miserable wretches, who were either stretched in irrecoverable intoxication on the floor, or prowling about, like beasts of prey, in search of plunder. The sofas, drawers, and other [Pg 48] articles of furniture, the due arrangement of which had cost so much thought and pains, were now broken into a thousand pieces, and scattered in confusion around me. Some of the geese and other poultry, escaped from their confinement, were cackling in the cuddy; while a solitary pig, wandering from its sty in the forecastle, was ranging at large in undisturbed possession of the Brussels carpet that covered one of the cabins. Glad to retire from a scene so cheerless and affecting, and rendered more dismal by the smoke which was oozing up from below, I returned to the poop, where I again found, amongst the few officers that remained, Capt. Cobb, Colonel Fearon, Lieuts. Ruxton, Booth, and Evans, superintending, with unabated zeal, the removal of the rapidly diminishing sufferers, as the boats successively arrived to carry them off.

The alarm and impatience of the people increased in a high ratio as the night advanced; and our fears, amid the surrounding darkness, were fed as much by the groundless or exaggerated reports of the timid as by the real and evident approach of the fatal crisis itself. With a view to ensure a greater probability of being discovered by those in [Pg 49] the boats, some of the more collected and hardy soldiers (for I think almost all the sailors had already effected their escape) took the precaution to tie towels and such like articles round their heads, previously to their committing themselves to the water.

As the boats were nearly three-quarters of an hour absent between each trip—which period was necessarily spent by those in the wreck in a state of fearful inactivity—abundant opportunity was afforded for collecting the sentiments of many of the unhappy men around me; some of whom, after remaining perhaps for a while in silent abstraction, would suddenly burst forth, as if awakened from some terrible dream to a still more frightful reality, into a long train of loud and desponding lamentation, that gradually subsided into its former stillness.

It was during those trying intervals of rest that religious instruction and consolation appeared to be the most required and the most acceptable. Some there were who endeavoured to dispense it agreeably to the visible wants and feelings of the earnest hearers. On one of those occasions, especially, the officer to whom I have already alluded was entreated to pray. His prayer [Pg 50] was short, but was frequently broken by the exclamations of assent to some of its confessions, that were wrung from the afflicted hearts of his auditors.

I know not in what manner, under those circumstances, spiritual hope or comfort could have been ministered to my afflicted companions by those who regard works, either wholly or partly, as the means of propitiating divine justice, rather than the evidence and fruits of that faith which pacifies the conscience and purifies the heart. But in some few cases, at least, where the individuals deplored the want of time for repentance and good works, I well remember that no arguments tended to soothe their troubled minds but those which went directly to assure them of the freeness and fulness of that grace which is not refused, even in the eleventh hour, to the very chief of sinners. And if any of those to whom I now allude have been spared to read this record of their feelings in the prospect of death, it will be well for them to keep solemnly in mind the vows they then took upon them, and to seek to improve that season of probation which they so earnestly besought, and which has been so mercifully extended to them, — by [Pg 51] humbly and incessantly applying for accessions of that faith which they are sensible removed the terrors of their awakened consciences, and can alone enable them henceforward to live in a sober, righteous, and godly manner, and thereby give the only unquestionable proof of their love to God, and their interest in the great salvation of His Son Jesus Christ.

If, on reading this imperfect narrative, [7] any persons beyond the immediate circle of my companions in misery (for within it I can safely declare that there were no indications of ridicule) should affect to despise, as contemptible or unsoldierlike, the humble devotional exercises to which I have now referred, I should like to assure them, that although they were undoubtedly commenced and prosecuted much more with an eternal than a temporal object in view, yet they also subserved the important purpose of restoring order and composure amongst a certain limited class of soldiers, at moments when mere military appeals had ceased to operate. [Pg 52]

I must state that, in general, it was not those most remarkable for their fortitude who evinced either a precipitancy to depart, or a desire to remain very long behind — the older and cooler soldiers appearing to possess too much regard for their officers, as well as for their individual credit, to take their hasty departure at a very early period of the day, and too much wisdom and resolution to hesitate to the very last.

But it was not till the close of this mournful tragedy that backwardness, rather than impatience, to adopt the perilous and only means of escape that offered, became generally discernible on the part of the unhappy remnant still on board, and that made it not only imperative on Captain Cobb to reiterate his threats, as well as his entreaties, that not an instant should be lost, but seemed to render it expedient for one of the officers of the troops, who had expressed his intention of remaining to the last, to limit, in the hearing of those around him, the period of his own stay. Seeing, however, between nine and ten o'clock, that some individuals were consuming the precious moments by obstinately hesitating to proceed, while others were making the inadmissible request [Pg 53] to be lowered down as the women had been, learning from the boatmen that the wreck, which was already nine or ten feet below the ordinary water mark, had sunk two feet lower since their last trip; and calculating, besides, that the two boats then under the stern, with that which was in sight on its return from the brig, would suffice for the conveyance of all who seemed in a condition to remove; the three remaining officers of the 31st regiment seriously prepared to take their departure.

As I cannot perhaps convey to you so correct an idea of the condition of others as by describing my own feelings and situation under the same circumstances, I shall make no apology for detailing the manner of my individual escape, which will sufficiently mark that of many hundreds that preceded it. The spanker-boom of so large a ship as the *Kent*, which projects, I should think, 16 or 18 feet over the stern, rests on ordinary occasions about 19 or 20 feet above the water; but in the position in which we were placed, from the great height of the sea, and the consequent pitching of the ship, it was frequently lifted to a height not less than 30 or 40 feet from the surface. [Pg 54]

To reach the rope, therefore, that hung from its extremity was an operation that seemed to require the aid of as much dexterity of hand as steadiness of head. For it was not only the nervousness of creeping along the boom itself, or the extreme difficulty of afterwards seizing on and sliding down by the rope that we had to dread, and that had occasioned the loss of some valuable lives by deterring men from adopting this mode of escape; but as the boat, which one moment was probably close under the boom, might be carried the next, by the force of the waves, 15 or 20 yards away from it, the unhappy individual, whose best calculations were thus defeated, was generally left swinging for some time in mid-air, if he was not repeatedly plunged several feet under water, or dashed with dangerous violence against the sides of the returning boat — or, what not unfrequently happened, was forced to let go his hold of the rope altogether. As there seemed, however, no alternative, I did not hesitate, notwithstanding my comparative inexperience and awkwardness in such a situation, to throw my legs across the perilous spar; and with a heart extremely grateful that [Pg 55] such means of deliverance, dangerous as they appeared, were still extended to me; and more grateful still that I had been enabled, in common with others, to discharge my honest duty to my sovereign and to my fellow-soldiers, I proceeded,—after confidently committing my spirit, the great object of my solicitude, into the keeping of Him who had formed and redeemed it,—to creep slowly forward, feeling at every step the increasing difficulty of my situation. On getting nearly to the end of the boom, the young officer whom I followed and myself were met with a squall of wind and rain so violent as to make us fain to embrace closely the slippery stick (without attempting for some minutes to make any progress), and to excite our apprehension that we must relinquish all hope of reaching the rope. But our fears were disappointed; and after resting for a little while at the boom end, while my companion was descending to the boat, which he did not find until he had been plunged once or twice over head in the water, I prepared to follow; and instead of lowering myself, as many had imprudently done, at the moment when the boat was inclining towards us—and consequently being [Pg 56] unable to descend the whole distance before it again receded,—I calculated that while the boat was retiring I ought to commence my descent, which would probably be completed by the time the returning wave brought it underneath; by which means I was, I believe, almost the only officer or soldier who reached the boat without being either severely bruised or immersed in the water.

But my good friend Colonel Fearon had not been so fortunate; for after swinging for some time, and being repeatedly struck against the side of the boat, and at one time drawn completely under it, he was at last so utterly exhausted that he must instantly have let go his hold of the rope and perished, had not some one in the boat seized him by the hair of the head, and dragged him into it, almost senseless and alarmingly bruised.

Captain Cobb, in his resolution to be the last, if possible, to quit his ship, and in his generous anxiety for the preservation of every life entrusted to his charge, refused to seek the boat until he again endeavoured to urge onward the few still around him, who seemed struck dumb and powerless with [Pg 57] dismay. [8] But finding all his entreaties fruitless, and hearing the guns, whose tackle was burst asunder by the advancing flames, successively exploding in the hold into which they had fallen, this gallant officer, after having nobly pursued, for the preservation of others, a course of exertion that has been rarely equalled either in its duration or difficulty, at last felt it right to provide for his own safety by laying hold on the topping-lift or rope that connects the driver boom with the mizentop, and thereby getting over the heads of the infatuated men who occupied the boom, unable to go either backward or forward, and ultimately dropping himself into the water.

The means of escape, however, did not cease to be presented to the unfortunate individuals above referred to, long after Captain Cobb took his departure; since one of the boats persevered in keeping its station under the *Kent's* stern, not only after all [Pg 58] expostulation and entreaty with those on board had foiled, but until the flames, bursting forth from the cabin windows, rendered it impossible to remain without inflicting the greatest cruelty on the individuals that manned it. But even on the return of the boat in question to the *Cambria*, with the single soldier who availed himself of it, did Captain Cook, with characteristic jealousy, refuse to allow it to come alongside until he learned that it was commanded by the spirited young officer, Mr. Thomson, [9] whose indefatigable exertions during the whole day were to him a sufficient proof that all had been done that could be done for the deliverance of those individuals.

THE MAGAZINE EXPLODED.

The same beneficent Providence which had been so wonderfully exerted for the preservation of hundreds, was pleased, by a still more striking and unquestionable display of power and goodness, to avert the fate of a portion of those few who, we had all too much reason to fear, were doomed to destruction. It would appear—for the poor men themselves give an extremely confused, [Pg 61] [Pg 60] [Pg 59] though I am persuaded not a wilfully false account of themselves—that shortly after the departure of the last boat they were driven by the flames to seek shelter on the chains, where they stood until the masts fell overboard, to which they then clung for some hours, in a state of horror that no language can describe; until they were, most providentially, I may say miraculously, discovered and picked up by Captain Bibbey, the humane commander of the *Caroline*, a vessel on its passage from Egypt to Liverpool, who happened, to see the explosion at a great distance, and instantly made all sail in the direction whence it proceeded. Along with the fourteen men thus miraculously preserved were three others, who had expired before the arrival of the *Caroline* to their rescue. [10] [Pg 62]

The men on their return to their regiment expressed themselves in terms of the liveliest gratitude for the affectionate attentions they received on board the *Caroline*, from Captain Bibbey, who considerately remained till daylight close to the wreck, in the hope that some others might still be found clinging to it—an act of humanity which, it will appear on the slightest reflection, would have been madness in Captain Cook, in the peculiar situation of the *Cambria*, to have attempted.

But when I recollect the lamentable state of exhaustion to which that portion of the crew were reduced, who unshrinkingly performed to the last their arduous and perilous duties,—and that out of the three boats that remained afloat, one was only prevented from sinking, towards the close of the night, by having the hole in its bottom repeatedly stuffed with soldiers' jackets, while the other two were rendered inefficient, the one by having its bow completely stove, and the second by being half filled with water, and the thwarts so torn as to make it necessary to lash the oars to the boat's ribs,—I must believe that, by those who thus laboured, all was done that humanity could possibly [Pg 63] demand, or intrepidity effect, for the preservation of every individual.

Quitting, for a moment, the subject of the wreck, I would advert to what was in the meantime taking place on board the *Cambria*. I cannot, however, pretend to give you any adequate idea of the feelings of hope or despair that alternately flowed, like a tide, in the breasts of the unhappy females on board the brig, during the many hours of torturing suspense in which several of them were unavoidably held respecting the fate of their husbands,—feelings which were inconceivably excited, rather than soothed, by the idle and erroneous rumours occasionally conveyed to them regarding the state of the *Kent*. But still less can I attempt to portray the alternate pictures of awful joy and of wild distraction exhibited by the sufferers (for both parties for the moment seemed equally to suffer), as the terrible truth was communicated that they and their children were indeed left husbandless and fatherless; or as the objects from whom they had feared they were for ever severed, suddenly rushed into their arms. But these feelings of delight, whatever may have been their intensity, were speedily [Pg 64] chastened, and the attention of all arrested, by the last tremendous spectacle of destruction.

After the arrival of the last boat the flames, which had spread along the upper deck and poop, ascended with the rapidity of lightning to the masts and rigging, forming one general conflagration, that illumined the heavens to an immense distance, and was strongly reflected by several objects on board the brig. The flags of distress, hoisted in the morning, were seen for a considerable time waving amid the flames, until the masts to which they were suspended successively fell like stately steeples over the ship's side. At last, about half-past one o'clock in the morning, the devouring element having communicated to the magazine, the explosion was seen, and the blazing fragments of the once magnificent *Kent* were instantly hurried, like so many rockets, high into the air; [11] leaving, in the comparative darkness that succeeded, the deathful scene of that disastrous day floating before the mind like some feverish dream. [Pg 65]

Shortly afterwards, the brig, which had been gradually making sail, was running at the rate of nine or ten miles an hour towards the nearest port. I would here endeavour to render my humble tribute of admiration and gratitude to that gallant and excellent individual, who, under God, was undoubtedly the chief instrument of our deliverance; if I were not sensible that testimony has been already borne to his heroic and humane efforts, in a manner much more commensurate with, and from quarters reflecting infinitely greater honour upon his merits, than the feeble expressions of them which I should be able to record. [12] I trust you will keep in mind that Captain Cook's generous intentions and exertions must have proved utterly unavailing for the preservation of so many lives, had they not been most nobly and unremittingly supported by those of his mate and crew, as well as of the numerous passengers on board his brig. While the former, only eight in number, were usefully and necessarily employed in working the vessel, the sturdy Cornish miners and York [Pg 66] shire smelters, on the approach of the different boats, took their perilous stations on the chains, where they put forth the great muscular strength with which Heaven had endowed them, in dexterously seizing, at each successive heave of the sea, on some of the exhausted people, and dragging them up on deck.

Nor did their kind assistance terminate there. They and the gentlemen connected with them cheerfully opened their ample stores of clothes and provisions, which they liberally dispensed to the naked and famished sufferers; they surrendered their beds to the helpless women and children, and seemed, in short, during the whole of our passage to England, to take no other delight than in ministering to all our wants.

Although, after the first burst of mutual gratulation, and of becoming acknowledgment of the divine mercy for our unlooked-for deliverance, had subsided, none of us felt disposed to much interchange of thought, each being rather inclined to wrap himself up in his own reflections; yet we did not, during the first night, view with the alarm it warranted, the extreme misery and danger [Pg 67] to which we were still exposed, by being crowded together, in a gale of wind, with upwards of 600 human beings, in a small brig of 200 tons, at a distance, too, of several hundred miles from any accessible port. Our little cabin, which was only calculated, under ordinary circumstances, for the accommodation of eight or ten persons, was now made to contain nearly eighty individuals, many of whom had no sitting room, and even some of the ladies no room to lie down. Owing to the continued violence of the gale, and to the bulwarks on one side of the brig having been driven in, the sea beat so incessantly over our deck as to render it necessary that the hatches should only be lifted up between the returning waves, to prevent absolute suffocation below, where the men were so closely packed together that the steam arising from their respiration excited at one time an apprehension that the vessel was on fire; while the impurity of the air they were inhaling became so marked, that the lights occasionally carried down amongst them were almost instantly extinguished. Nor was the condition of the hundreds who covered the deck less wretched than that of their com [Pg 68] rades below; since they were obliged night and day to stand shivering, in their wet and nearly naked state, ankle deep in water: [13]—some of the older children and females were thrown into fits, while the infants were piteously crying for that nourishment which their nursing mothers were no longer able to give them. [14]

Our only hope amid these great and accumulating miseries was that the same compassionate Providence which had already so marvellously interposed in our behalf would not permit the favourable wind to abate or change until we reached some friendly port; for we were all convinced that a delay of a very few days longer at sea must inevitably involve us in famine, pestilence, and a complication of the most dreadful evils. Our hopes were not disappointed. The gale continued with even increasing violence; and our able captain, crowding all sail, at [Pg 69] the risk of carrying away his masts, so nobly urged his vessel onward, that in the afternoon of Thursday, the 3rd, the delightful exclamation from aloft was heard, "Land ahead!" In the evening we descried the Scilly lights; and running rapidly along the Cornish coast, we joyfully cast anchor in Falmouth harbour, at about half-past twelve o'clock at night.

On reviewing the various proximate causes to which so many human beings owed their deliverance from a combination of dangers as remarkable for their duration as they were appalling in their aspect, it is impossible, I think, not to discover and gratefully acknowledge, in the beneficence of their arrangement, the overruling providence of that blessed Being, who is sometimes pleased, in His mysterious operations, to produce the same effect from causes apparently different; and on the other hand, as in our own case, to bring forth results the most opposite, from one and the same cause.

For there is no doubt that the heavy rolling of our ship, occasioned by the violent gale, which was the real origin of all our disasters, contributed also most essentially to our subsequent preservation; since, had not Captain Cobb been [Pg 70] enabled, by the greatness of the swell, to introduce speedily through the gun ports the immense quantity of water that inundated the hold, and thereby checked for so long a time the fury of the flames, the *Kent* must unquestionably have been consumed before many, perhaps before any, of those on board could have found shelter in the *Cambria*. [15]

But it is unnecessary to dwell on an insulated fact like this, amidst a concatenation of circumstances, all leading to the same conclusion, and so closely bound together as to force us to confess, that if a single link in the chain had been withdrawn or withheld, we must all most probably have perished.

The *Cambria*, which had been, it seems, unaccountably detained in port nearly a month after the period assigned for her departure, was early on the morning of the fatal calamity pursuing at a great distance ahead of us the same course with ourselves; but her bulwarks on the weather side having been suddenly driven in, by a heavy sea breaking over her quarter, Captain Cook, in his anxiety to give ease to his labouring [Pg 71] vessel, was induced to go completely out of his course by throwing the brig on the opposite tack, by which means alone he was brought in sight of us. Not to dwell on the unexpected, but not unimportant facts of the flames having been mercifully prevented, for eleven hours, from either communicating with the magazine forward, or the great spirit room abaft, or even coming into contact with the tiller ropes—any of which circumstances would evidently have been fatal,—I would remark that, until the *Cambria* hove in sight, we had not discovered any vessel whatever for several days previous; nor did we afterwards see another until we entered the chops of the Channel. It is to be remembered, too, that had the *Cambria*, with her small crew, been homeward instead of outward bound, her scanty remainder of provisions, under such circumstances, would hardly have sufficed to form a single meal for our vast assemblage; or if, instead of having her lower deck completely clear, she had been carrying out a full cargo, there would not have been time, under the pressure of the danger and the violence of the gale, to throw the cargo overboard, and certainly, with it, not suffi [Pg 72] cient space in the brig to contain one-half of our number.

When I reflect, besides, on the disastrous consequences that must have followed if, during our passage home, which was performed in a period most unusually short, the wind had either veered round a few points, or even partially subsided—which must have produced a scene of horror on board more terrible if possible than that from which we had escaped; and above all, when I recollect the extraordinary fact, and that which seems to have the most forcibly struck the whole of us, that we had not been above an hour in Falmouth harbour, when the wind, which had all along been blowing from the south-west, suddenly chopped round to the opposite quarter of the compass, and continued uninterruptedly for several days afterwards to blow strongly from the north-east,—one cannot help concluding that he who sees nothing of a Divine Providence in our preservation must be lamentably and wilfully blind to "the majesty of the Lord."

In the course of the morning we all prepared, with thankful and joyful hearts, to place our feet on the shores of Old England.

The ladies, always destined to form our [Pg 73] vanguard, were the first to disembark, and were met on the beach by immense crowds of the inhabitants, who appeared to have been attracted thither less by idle curiosity than from the sincerest desire to alleviate in every possible manner their manifest sufferings.

The sailors and soldiers, cold, wet, and almost naked, quickly followed; the whole forming, in their haggard looks and the endless variety of their costume, an assemblage at once as melancholy and grotesque as it is possible to conceive. So eager did the people appear to be to pour out upon us the full current of their sympathies, that shoes, hats, and other articles of urgent necessity were presented to several of the officers and men before they had even quitted the point of disembarkation. And in the course of the day, many of the officers and soldiers, and almost all of the females, were partaking, in the private houses of individuals, of the most liberal and needful hospitality.

But this flow of compassion and kindness did not cease with the impulse of the more immediate occasion that had called it forth. For a meeting of the inhabitants was afterwards held, where subscriptions in clothes and money to a large amount were collected [Pg 74] for the relief of the numerous sufferers. The women and children, whose wants seemed to demand their first care, were speedily furnished with comfortable clothing, and the poor widows and orphans with decent mourning. Depositories of shirts, shoes, stockings, etc., were formed for the supply of the officers and private passengers; and the sick and wounded in the hospital were made the recipients, not only of all those kindly attentions and medical assistance that could remove or soothe their temporal suffering, but were also invited to partake freely of the most judicious spiritual consolation and instruction. This march of charity was conducted by the ladies of Falmouth, who were zealously accompanied on it by the whole body, in the vicinity, of that peculiar sect of Christians, who have ever been as remarkable for their unassuming pretensions and consistent conduct, as for unostentatiously standing in the front ranks of every good work. And so strong is the reason which I, in particular, have to associate in my mind all that is sincere, considerate, and charitable with the society of Friends, that the very badge of Quakerism will, I trust, henceforward prove a full and [Pg 75] sufficient passport to the best feelings of my heart.

On the first Sunday after our arrival, Colonel Fearon, followed by all his officers and men, and accompanied by Captain Cobb, and the officers and private passengers of his late ship, hastened to prostrate themselves before the throne of the Heavenly grace, to pour out the public expression of their thanksgiving to their almighty Preserver. The scene was deeply impressive; and it is earnestly to be hoped that many a poor fellow who listened, perhaps for the first time in his life, with unquestionable sincerity and humility to the voice of instruction, will be found steadily prosecuting, in the strength of God, the good resolutions that he may on that solemn occasion have formed, until he be able to say, as one of the greatest generals of antiquity did, that "it was good for him to have been afflicted; for before he was afflicted he went astray, but that afterwards he was not ashamed to keep God's word."

In the course of a few days the private passengers and most of the sailors of our party were dispersed in various directions; and the troops, after having incurred to the [Pg 76] excellent inhabitants of

Falmouth, and the adjacent towns, a debt of gratitude which none of them can ever hope to repay, were embarked for Chatham.

I think you must be already sensible that the circumstances of our situation on board the *Kent* did not enable us conscientiously to save a single article, either of public or private property, from the flames; indeed, the only thing I preserved—with the exception of forty or fifty sovereigns, which I hastily tied up in my pocket hand-kerchief, and put into my wife's hands, at the moment she was lifted into the boat, as a provision for herself and her companions against the temporary want to which they might be exposed on some foreign shore—was the pocket compass, which you yourself presented to me. [16]

But I would have you to be assured, that the total abandonment of individual interests on the part of the officers of the ship, and of the 31st regiment, was occasioned by no want of self-possession, nor even, in all cases, of opportunities to attend to them; but to a [Pg 77] sincere desire to avoid even the appearance of selfishness, at moments when the valuable lives of their sailors and soldiers were at stake. And this observation applies with still greater force to the senior officers in both services, whose cabins being upon the upper deck were accessible during the whole day; and where many portable articles of value were deposited, which could have been very easily carried off, had those officers been disposed to devote to their own concerns even a portion of that precious time, and of those active exertions, which they unremittingly applied to the performance of their professional duty.

Notwithstanding the unexpected length to which I have already extended this narrative, I cannot allow myself to close it without offering to my late companions on board the *Kent*, into whose hands it may possibly fall, a few very plain and simple observations, which I think worthy of their serious consideration, and the importance of which I desire to have deeply impressed upon my own mind. None of those soldiers who were in the habit of reading their Bibles can have failed to notice that faith in Jesus Christ, the Son of God, is therein made the [Pg 78] great pivot on which the salvation of man hinges; that the whole human race, without distinction of rank, nation, age, or sex, being justly exposed to the wrath of Almighty God, nothing but the precious blood of Christ, which was shed on the cross, can possibly atone for their sins; and that faith in this atonement can alone pacify the conscience, and awaken confidence towards God as a reconciled Father. If, therefore, "he that believeth in Christ shall be saved, and he that believeth not shall be damned," be the unequivocal language of Jehovah, either expressly declared or obviously implied in every page of that record which He has vouchsafed to us of His Son; is it not a question of the deepest concernment to every one professing any regard for divine revelation, whether he really understands and believes that record, and whether he is able to give, not only to others, but to himself, a reason of this hope that is in him?

From the influence of education or example, the absence of serious reflection, an attention to the outward ordinances of religion, a regard to many of the proprieties and decencies of life, and a forgetfulness that the religion of the Bible is a religion [Pg 79] of motives rather than one of observances, minds easily satisfied on such subjects may persuade themselves that they are spiritually alive while they are dead—that they are amongst the sincere disciples of the blessed Redeemer, and fully interested in His salvation, while they may have neither part nor lot in the matter. But if, at the hour of death, when all external support shall slide away, the soul shall be awakened to the consciousness of its real condition; if it should be made to see, on the one hand, the spirituality and exceeding breadth of the divine law, and be quickened, on the other, to a sense of its unnumbered transgressions; if the mercy of God out of Christ, in which so many vainly and vaguely trust, should become obscured by the inflexible justice and spotless holiness of His character and if the solitary spirit, as it is dragged towards the mysterious precipice, is made to hear, from a voice which it can no longer mistake, "Cursed is every one that continueth not in all things which are written in the book of the law to do them,"—how unspeakably miserable must be the condition of the man who thus discovers, for the first time, that the sand which he had all his lifetime been [Pg 80] mistaking for the "Rock of Ages" is now giving way under his feet, and that his soul must speedily sink into that state in which, "where the tree falleth, there it shall be;" where "he that is unjust, let him be unjust still;" and where there is "no work, nor device, nor knowledge," nor repentance.

But that I may not be misunderstood, or be supposed to favour principles of barren speculation, more delusive and dangerous to their possessors, and to the best interests of society, than absolute ignorance itself—I would remind the gallant men to whom I am now more especially addressing myself, that that faith which saves the soul not only "worketh" invariably "by love," and gradually "overcometh the world," but that "it is the gift of God," implanted in the heart by His Holy Spirit, even by that Spirit which is freely given to every one that earnestly asketh. And however unable the simple soldier may be to explain either the nature or the manner of its operation, he must not deceive himself into the persuasion that he is possessed of this precious grace unless he feels it bringing forth in his life and conversation the abundant fruits that necessarily spring from it, and that cannot [Pg 81] indeed be produced without it. He will be steady and zealous in the performance of duty, patient under fatigue and privation, sober amid temptation, calm but firm in the hour of danger, and respectfully obedient to his officers; he will honour his king, be content with his wages, and do harm to no man. His piety will be ardent but sober, his prayers will be earnest and frequent, but rather in secret than before men; he will not be contentious or disputatious, but rather desirous of instructing others by his example than by his precepts; letting his light so shine before them, in the simplicity of his motives, the uprightness of his actions, in his readiness to oblige, and by the whole tenor of his life, that they, seeing his good works, may be led, by the divine blessing, to acknowledge the reality and power and beauty of religion, and be induced in like manner to glorify his heavenly Father. In short, in comparison with his thoughtless comrades, he must not only aspire to become a better man, but, from the constraining motives of the gospel, struggle to be also in every essential respect a better soldier.

In conclusion, I would observe that if any class of men, more than another, ought [Pg 82] to be struck with awe and gratitude by the goodness and providence of God, it is they who go down to the sea in ships, and see His wonders in the great deep; or if any ought to familiarize their minds with death and its solemn consequences, it is surely soldiers, "whose very business it is to die." May all those then, especially, who thus possessed the privilege, but rarely granted, of being allowed, in the full vigour of health, and in the absence of all the bustle and excitement of battle, to contemplate, from the very brink of eternity, the awful realities that reign within it, as many of their departing comrades were hurried through its dreadful portals, be now led, in the respite which has been given them, to remember that this alone is the accepted time, and this the day of salvation; for while some may defer the subject "to a more convenient season," the message may come forth, at an hour when it is least expected, "This night thy soul shall be required of thee." [Pg 83] The foregoing narrative may be fitly supplemented by some particulars [17] of the events occurring after the departure of the *Cambria* from the scene of the wreck:—

"About twelve o'clock the watch of the barque *Caroline*, on her passage from Alexandria to Liverpool, observed a light on the horizon, and knew it at once to be a ship on fire. There was a heavy sea on, but the captain, instantly setting his maintop-gallant-sail, ran down towards the spot. About one, the sky becoming brighter, a sudden jet of vivid light shot up; but they were too distant to hear the explosion. In half-an-hour the *Caroline* could see the wreck of a large vessel lying head to the wind. The ribs and frame timbers, marking the outlines of double ports and quarter-galleries, showed that the burning skeleton was that of a first-class Indiaman. Every other external feature was gone; she was burnt nearly to the water's edge, but still floated, pitching majestically as she rose and fell on the long rolling swell of the bay. The vessel looked like an immense cage of charred basket-work filled with flame, that here and there blazed brighter at intervals. Above, and [Pg 84] far to leeward, there was a vast drifting cloud of curling smoke spangled with millions of sparks and burning flakes, and scattered by the wind over the sky and waves.

"As the *Caroline* approached, part of a mast and some spars, rising and falling, were observed grinding under the weather-quarter of the wreck, having got entangled with the keel or rudder irons, and thus attaching it to the hull of the vessel. The *Caroline*, coming down swift before the wind, was in a few minutes brought across the bows of the *Kent.* At that moment a shout was heard as if from the very centre of the fire, and the same instant several figures were observed clinging to a mast. The sea was heavy, and the wreck threatened every moment to disappear. The *Caroline* was hove-to to leeward, in order to avoid the showers of flakes and sparks, and to intercept any boats or rafts. The mate and four seamen pushed off in the jolly-boat, through a sea covered with floating spars, chests, and furniture, that threatened to crush or overwhelm the boat. When within a few yards of the stern, they caught sight of the first living thing—a wretched man clinging to a [Pg 85] spar close under the ship's counter. Every time the stern-frame rose with the swell he was suspended above the water, and scorched by the long keen tongues of pure flame that now came darting through the gun-room ports. Each time this torture came the man shrieked with agony; the next moment the surge came and buried him under the wave, and he was silent. The *Caroline's* men, defying the fire, pulled close to him, but just as their hands were stretching towards him (latterly the poor wretch had been silent), the rope or spar was snapped by the fire, and he sank for ever.

"The men then, carefully backing, carried off six other of the nearest men from the mast. The small boat, only eighteen feet long, would not hold more than eleven persons, and indeed, as it was, was nearly swamped by a heavy wave. In half-an-hour the boat bravely returned, and took off six more.

"The mate, fearing the vessel was going down, and that the masts would be swallowed in the vortex, redoubled his efforts to get a third time to the wreck. While struggling with a head sea, and before the boat could reach the mast, the end came. The fiery [Pg 86] mass settled like a red-hot coal into the waves, and disappeared for ever. The sky grew instantly dark, a dense shroud of black smoke lingered over the grave of the ship, and instead of the crackle of burning timbers and the flutter of flames, there spread the ineffable stillness of death.

"As the last gleam flickered out, Mr. Wallen, the mate of the *Caroline*, with great quickness of thought set the spot by a star. Then, in spite of the danger in the darkness of floating wreck, he resolved to wait quietly till daylight, and ordered his men to shout repeatedly to cheer any who might be still floating on stray spars. For a long time no one answered; at last a feeble cry came, and the *Caroline's* sailors returned it loudly and gladly. What joy that faint cry must have brought to those friendly ears! With what joy must the boat-men's shout have been received!

WHEN DAY BROKE THE MAST WAS VISIBLE.

"When the day broke the mast was visible, and four motionless men could be seen among its cordage and top-work. They seemed dead, but as the boat neared, two of them feebly raised their heads and stretched out their arms. When taken into the boat, they were found to be faint and almost dead from [Pg 89] [Pg 88] [Pg 87] the cold and wet, and the many hours they had been half under water. The other two were stone dead. One had bound himself firmly to the spar, and lay as if asleep, with his arms around it, and his head upon it, as if it had been a pillow. The other stood half upright between the cheeks of the mast, his face fixed in the direction of the boat, his arms still extended. They were both left on the spar. One of the Indiaman's empty boats was also found drifting a short distance off. The wind beginning to freshen and a gale coming on, it was all the jolly-boat could do to rejoin the *Caroline*. There could be no doubt that when the *Caroline* hove-to and luffed under the lee of the *Kent*, it must have passed men drifting to leeward on detached spars. They of course all perished in the rising storm.

"A piece of plate was presented to Captain Cook, of the *Cambria*, by the officers and passengers of the *Kent*, and the Duke of York publicly thanked him for his humane zeal and promptitude. The Secretary of War (Lord Palmerston) authorized a sum of five hundred pounds to be given to the captain and crew of the *Cambria*, and the agents of the ship were also paid two hundred and [Pg 90] eighty-seven pounds for provisions, two hundred and eighty-seven pounds for passengers' diet, and five hundred pounds for demurrage. The East India Company awarded six hundred pounds to Captain Cook, one hundred pounds to the first mate, fifty pounds to the second mate, ten pounds each to the nine men of the crew, fifteen pounds each to the twenty-six miners, and one hundred pounds to the ten chief miners for extra stores, to make their voyage out more comfortable. The Royal Exchange Assurance gave Captain Cook fifty pounds, and his officers and crew fifty pounds. The subscribers to Lloyds voted him a present of one hundred pounds; the Royal Humane Society awarded him an honorary medallion; and the underwriters at Liverpool were also prominent in their liberality."

FOOTNOTES:

[1] Captain Cobb, with great forethought, ordered the deck to be scuttled forward, with a view to draw the fire in that direction, knowing that between it and the magazine were several tiers of water-casks; while he hoped that the wet sails, etc., thrown into the after-hold, would prevent the fire from communicating with the spirit-room abaft.

[2] The late Lady MacGregor, and the late Mrs. Pringle, of Yair, Whytbank, Selkirk, N.B., who are also mentioned in the letter on page **23** .

[3] This bottle, left in the cabin, was cast into the sea by the explosion that destroyed the *Kent*. About nineteen months afterwards the following notice appeared in a Barbadoes (West Indian) newspaper: —

"A bottle was picked up on Saturday, the 30th September, at Bathsheba (a bathing-place on the west of Barbadoes), by a gentleman who was bathing there, who, on breaking it, found the melancholy account of the fate of the ship *Kent*, contained in a folded paper written with pencil, but scarcely legible." The words of the letter were then given, and a facsimile of it will be found on the next page. The letter itself, taken from the bottle thickly encrusted with shells and seaweed, was returned to the writer when he arrived, shortly after its discovery, at Barbadoes, as Lieut.-Colonel of the 93rd Highlanders, and the interesting relic is still preserved by his son (at that time called "little Rob Roy"), who is not mentioned in the letter, but was saved as related in page **33** .

[4] Two shipwrights, dismissed from their situation because they would not work on Sunday, were employed by the father of a friend of the writer. He engaged them to build their first vessel, the *Cambria*, and this was her first voyage, starting from Deptford before the *Kent* sailed from Gravesend.

Captain Cook many years afterwards commanded in the disastrous "Niger Expedition." He was a splendid sailor, and a humble Christian, whose death-bed, long years after, was attended by the youngest passenger he had helped to save from the burning *Kent*.

[5] I was afterwards informed by one of the passengers on board the *Cambria* — for from the great height of the Indiaman we had not the opportunity of making a similar observation — that when both vessels happened to be at the same time in the trough of the sea, the *Kent* was entirely concealed by the intervening waves from the deck of the *Cambria*.

[6] "The *Rob Roy* Canoe on the Jordan" (Murray) gives some other experiences of watery dangers in after life.

[7] This narrative has been translated into the French, Spanish, Swedish, Italian, German, and Russian languages, and the author (born March 16, 1787) still enjoys good health (1880) while writing the preface to this edition, of which a *facsimile* is given at the beginning of the book.

[8] Some of those men who were necessarily left behind, having previously conducted themselves with great propriety and courage, I think it but justice to express my belief that the same difficulties which had nearly proved fatal to Captain Cobb's personal escape were probably found to be insurmountable by landsmen, whose coolness, unaccompanied with dexterity and experience, might not be available to them in their awful situation.

[9] I ought to state that the exertions of Mr. Muir, third mate, were also most conspicuous during the whole day.

[10] See page **83** . — One of the men saved after the explosion (which had burned off both his feet) was met thirty years afterwards by the individual who was first saved in the *Cambria*. This man was wheeling himself in a go-cart on the race-ground at Lanark, dressed in sailor's costume, and selling papers with a picture of the *Kent* upon them and some doggerel verses below. As honorary secretary of the "Open-Air Mission" (which provides preachers for streets in towns, and for races and fairs in the country), the "first saved" from the wreck and burning then preached the Gospel to the "last saved" from the scorched embers, and to a large and motley crowd, all of whom will assuredly meet once more "at that day."

[11] Besides 500 barrels of gunpowder, there was on board several hundredweight of highly explosive percussion powder. The brig was about three miles distant when the *Kent* exploded.

[12] Captain Cook afterwards rendered distinguished services in the Niger expedition, and died in London a true Christian sailor, after several visits from one he had helped to save.

[13] In addition to those who were naked on board the *Kent* at the moment the alarm of fire was heard, several individuals afterwards threw off their clothes to enable them the more easily to swim to the boats.

[14] One of the soldiers' wives was delivered of a child about an hour or two after her arrival on board the brig. Both survived, and the child received the appropriate name of "Cambria."

[15] There were lost in the destruction of the *Kent*, 54 soldiers, 1 woman, and 20 children, belonging to the 31st Regiment; 1 seaman and 5 boys—total, 81 individuals.

[16] A little Testament was also saved. Only one officer's sword was saved, and that belonged to him who afterwards led the 31st regiment in the battles on the Sutlej.

[17] From *All the Year Round.*